GOD AND ART

A Biblical Vision for Creativity and Beauty

PHILLIP J. RICHMOND

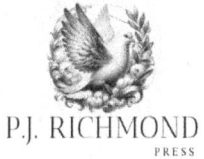

P.J. RICHMOND
PRESS

Please consider writing a review!

DEDICATION

*This book is dedicated to the Creator and the Artist of all,
God Almighty, who made us in His image, and gave us the
gift of art. To Him be the glory and the praise forever and
ever. Amen.*

*This book is also dedicated to all the artists and art lovers,
who use their gifts and talents, their resources and time,
their imagination and emotions, their words and actions, to
create and appreciate art that honors God and blesses
others. May God fill you with His Spirit, and guide you
with His wisdom. May God make you more like His Son,
and prepare you for His kingdom. May God bless your art
and your lives, and use them for His glory and the good of
others. Amen.*

Also By Phillip J. Richmond

The Spiritual Awakening

Supernatural Warfare Prayers

The Path to a Godly Life

Self-Deliverance Made Easy

The Rapture

Deepening Faith

The Meaning of Salvation

Overcoming Trauma From Rape

How to Stop Masturbation

God's Solution For Your Problems

Breaking Free

Exploring The Secrets of Pets and The Afterlife

The Problem of Grief

Shine Bright

How to Be A Better Partner

The Act of Being Single

Quick Wit, Confident Speech

CONTENTS

DEDICATION II

INTRODUCTION 1

CHAPTER 1 5

    God as the Ultimate Artist and the Source of All

    Beauty 5

CHAPTER 2 23

    Art as a Form of Worship and Witness 23

CHAPTER 3 29

    Art as a Means of Transformation and Healing 29

CHAPTER 4 37

    Art as a Tool for Service and Stewardship 37

CHAPTER 5 45

    Art as a Celebration of Diversity and Unity 45

CONCLUSION 53

    How to Cultivate a Biblical Vision for Creativity and

    Beauty 53

SPECIAL BONUS 57

In the beginning God created the

heavens and the earth.

Genesis 1:1

INTRODUCTION

Art is one of the most universal and powerful forms of human expression. Art is the product of human creativity, imagination, and skill. Art is the manifestation of human emotions, thoughts, and experiences. Art is the communication of human ideas, values, and messages. Art is the celebration of human beauty, diversity, and culture.

Art can take many forms, such as painting, sculpture, music, literature, poetry, drama, dance, film, photography, and more. Art can serve many purposes, such as entertainment, education, inspiration, persuasion, therapy, and more. Art can have many effects, such as pleasure, joy, wonder, awe, curiosity, sadness, anger, fear, and more.

Art is not only a human activity, but also a divine gift. Art is not only a reflection of our humanity, but also a revelation of God's divinity. Art is not only a way of expressing ourselves, but also a way of experiencing God.

God is the ultimate artist and the source of all beauty. He created the world and everything in it with His wisdom, power, and love. He filled the world with His beauty and glory, and He invites us to enjoy and appreciate His creation. He made us in His image and likeness, and He gave us the ability and the desire to create and appreciate art. He speaks to us through His word and His Spirit, and He uses art to communicate His truth, grace, and love to us. He calls us to worship Him with all our heart, soul, mind, and strength, and He uses art to express our love, gratitude, and praise to Him.

In this book, we will explore the relationship between God and art, and how it affects our relationship with Him, ourselves, and others. We will discover what the Bible says about art, creativity, and beauty, and how it applies to our lives. We will learn how to cultivate a biblical vision for art, and how to use art for God's glory and our good.

We will divide this book into five chapters, each focusing on a different aspect of God and art. In chapter one, we will look at God as the ultimate artist and the source of all beauty. We will see how God reveals His beauty and glory through His creation, how He invites us to participate in His creativity and enjoy His artistry, and how He equips us with artistic gifts and talents to reflect His image and likeness. In chapter two, we will look at art as a form of worship and witness. We will see how art can express our love, gratitude, and praise to God, how art can communicate God's truth, grace, and love to others, and how art can inspire, challenge, and edify ourselves and others. In chapter three, we will look at art as a means of transformation and healing. We will see how art can help us grow in our knowledge and experience of God, how art can help us cope with our emotions, struggles, and wounds, and how art can help us restore our brokenness and wholeness in Christ. In chapter four, we will look at art as a tool for service and stewardship. We will see how art can serve God's purposes and plans for our lives and the world, how art can bless, support, and empower others in need, and how art can honor God with our resources, time, and talents. In chapter five, we will look at art as a celebration of diversity and unity. We will see how art can reflect and appreciate the diversity of God's creation and people, how art can foster and promote the unity of God's family and kingdom, and how art can anticipate and rejoice in the beauty of God's future and eternity.

My hope and prayer is that this book will help you to see God and art in a new light, and to experience divine intimacy in your relationships. I hope that this book will inspire you to create and appreciate art with a biblical perspective, and to use art as a way of loving God and others. I hope that this book will challenge you to grow in your artistic gifts and talents, and to use them for God's glory and your good. I hope that this book will bless you and others with God's beauty, truth, and love.

Let us begin our journey of exploring God and art, and let us pray that God will guide us, teach us, and transform us along the way. Amen.

CHAPTER 1

God as the Ultimate Artist and the Source of All Beauty

Have you ever marveled at the beauty and complexity of nature? Have you ever admired the colors and shapes of the flowers, the birds, and the butterflies? Have you ever gazed at the stars and the planets, and wondered how they came to be? Have you ever listened to the sounds of the wind, the waves, and the rain, and felt a sense of peace and awe?

If you have, then you have witnessed the art of God. God is the ultimate artist and the source of all beauty. He created the world and everything in it with His wisdom, power, and love. He filled the world with His beauty and glory, and He invites us to enjoy and appreciate His creation. He made us in His image and likeness, and He gave us the ability and the desire to create and appreciate art. He speaks to us through His word and His Spirit, and He uses art to communicate His truth, grace, and love to us. He calls us to worship Him with all our heart, soul, mind, and strength, and He uses art to express our love, gratitude, and praise to Him.

In this chapter, we will explore three aspects of God and art: how God reveals His beauty and glory through His creation, how God invites us to participate in His creativity and enjoy His artistry, and how God equips us with artistic gifts and talents to reflect His image and likeness.

How God Reveals His Beauty and Glory Through His Creation

The first thing we need to understand about God and art is that God is the ultimate artist and the source of all beauty. He is the one who created the world and everything in it with His wisdom, power, and love. He is the one who designed the laws of nature, the patterns of life, and the diversity of species. He is the one who painted the sky with the sun, the moon, and the stars. He is the one who sculpted the mountains, the valleys, and the oceans. He is the one who composed the music of the wind, the waves, and the rain. He is the one who wrote the story of history, redemption, and eternity.

The Bible tells us that God created the world and everything in it in six days, and that He saw that it was good (Genesis 1). The Bible also tells us that God created the world and everything in it for His own pleasure and glory (Revelation 4:11). The Bible also tells us that God created the world and everything in it to reveal His invisible attributes, such as His eternal power and divine nature (Romans 1:20).

God's creation is not only good, but also beautiful. God's creation is not only functional, but also aesthetic. God's creation is not only natural, but also supernatural. God's creation is not only physical, but also spiritual. God's creation is not only temporal, but also eternal.

God's creation is His art, and His art is His revelation. God reveals His beauty and glory through His creation, and He invites us to see, hear, touch, smell, and taste His art. He invites us to discover His wisdom, power, and love through His art. He invites us to experience His presence, grace, and joy through His art.

The psalmist David was one of the most artistic and expressive people in the Bible. He was a poet, a musician, a singer, and a dancer. He was also a lover of God and His creation. He wrote many psalms that praise God for His beauty and glory as revealed through His creation. For example, in Psalm 19, he wrote:

"The heavens proclaim the glory of God. The skies display his craftsmanship. Day after day they continue to speak; night after night they make him known. They speak without a sound or word; their voice is never heard. Yet their message has gone throughout the earth, and their words to all the world. God has made a home in the heavens for the sun. It bursts forth like a radiant bridegroom after his wedding. It rejoices like a great athlete eager to run the race. The sun rises at one end of the heavens and follows its course to the other end. Nothing can hide from its heat." (Psalm 19:1-6)

David saw God's beauty and glory in the heavens, the skies, the sun, and the stars. He saw God's art as a testimony of His greatness, majesty, and splendor. He saw God's art as a language that speaks to all people, in all places, and in all times. He saw God's art as a source of light, warmth, and life.

David also saw God's beauty and glory in the earth, the land, the sea, and the animals. He saw God's art as a display of His creativity, diversity, and generosity. He saw God's art as a gift that sustains, nourishes, and delights us. He saw God's art as a reflection of His character, nature, and attributes. For example, in Psalm 104, he wrote:

"O Lord, what a variety of things you have made! In wisdom you have made them all. The earth is full of your creatures. Here is the ocean, vast and wide, teeming with life of every kind, both large and small. See the ships sailing along, and Leviathan, which you made to play in the sea. They all depend on you to give them food as they need it. When you supply it, they gather it. You open your hand to feed them, and they are richly satisfied. But if you turn away from them, they panic. When you take away their breath, they die and turn again to dust. When you give them your breath, life is created, and you renew the face of the earth." (Psalm 104:24-30)

David saw God's beauty and glory in the ocean, the ships, the fish, and the Leviathan. He saw God's art as a demonstration of His power, sovereignty, and playfulness. He saw God's art as a reminder of His providence, care, and satisfaction. He saw God's art as a sign of His life, breath, and renewal.

God reveals His beauty and glory through His creation, and He invites us to see, hear, touch, smell, and taste His art. He invites us to discover His wisdom, power, and love through His art. He invites us to experience His presence, grace, and joy through His art. He invites us to worship Him, thank Him, and praise Him for His art.

How God Invites Us to Participate in His Creativity and Enjoy His Artistry

The second thing we need to understand about God and art is that God invites us to participate in His creativity and enjoy His artistry. He is not only the ultimate artist and the source of all beauty, but also the most generous and gracious host and teacher. He does not keep His art to Himself, but He shares it with us. He does not hide His art from us, but He reveals it to us. He does not limit His art to Himself, but He invites us to join Him in His art.

God invites us to participate in His creativity and enjoy His artistry in two ways: by creating art and by appreciating art.

God invites us to create art, because He made us in His image and likeness, and He gave us the ability and the desire to create and appreciate art. He gave us the gift of creativity, imagination, and skill, and He wants us to use them for His glory and our good. He gave us the gift of art, and He wants us to express ourselves, communicate with others, and worship Him through art.

The Bible tells us that God made us in His image and likeness, and that He gave us dominion over the earth and everything in it (Genesis 1:26-28). The Bible also tells us that God filled us with His Spirit, and that He gave us different gifts and talents according to His grace (1 Corinthians 12:4-11). The Bible also tells us that God prepared good works for us to do, and that He created us to do them (Ephesians 2:10).

One of the ways that we can exercise our dominion, use our gifts, and do our good works is by creating art. Art is one of the ways that we can reflect God's image and likeness, and glorify Him with our lives. Art is one of the ways that we can express our emotions, thoughts, and experiences, and share them with others. Art is one of the ways that we can communicate God's truth, grace, and love, and witness to others. Art is one of the ways that we can worship God with all our heart, soul, mind, and strength, and praise Him with our lips.

The Bible gives us many examples of people who created art for God's glory and their good. For example, in Exodus 31, we read about Bezalel and Oholiab, two craftsmen who were filled with the Spirit of God and given the skill and knowledge to make all kinds of artistic works for the tabernacle, the place where God dwelled among His people. They made the ark of the covenant, the table, the lampstand, the altar, the curtains, and the garments for the priests. They used gold, silver, bronze, wood, stone, fabric, and precious stones to create beautiful and meaningful objects that honored God and served His people.

Another example is in 2 Chronicles 2, we read about King Solomon, who was the wisest and richest king of Israel. He wanted to build a temple for the Lord, a place where God would dwell among His people. He hired skilled workers and craftsmen from Israel and other nations to make all kinds of artistic works for the temple. They used gold, silver, bronze, iron, wood, stone, fabric, and precious stones to create magnificent and splendid objects that honored God and served His people.

Another example is in Luke 1, we read about Mary, the mother of Jesus. She was a young and humble woman who was chosen by God to give birth to the Savior of the world. She responded to God's call with faith and obedience, and she praised God with a beautiful song of worship. She used words, melody, and poetry to create a heartfelt and meaningful expression of her love, gratitude, and joy to God.

These are just a few examples of people who created art for God's glory and their good. There are many more examples in the Bible and in history of people who used their artistic gifts and talents to serve God and others. God invites us to create art, because He made us in His image and likeness, and He gave us the ability and the desire to create and appreciate art. He invites us to use our creativity, imagination, and skill for His glory and our good. He invites us to express ourselves, communicate with others, and worship Him through art.

God also invites us to appreciate art, because He made us in His image and likeness, and He gave us the ability and the desire to create and appreciate art. He gave us the gift of perception, understanding, and enjoyment, and He wants us to use them for His glory and our good. He gave us the gift of art, and He wants us to see, hear, touch, smell, and taste His art.

The Bible tells us that God made us in His image and likeness, and that He gave us senses, intellect, and emotions (Genesis 2:7, 21-23). The Bible also tells us that God gave us wisdom, knowledge, and discernment (Proverbs 2:6-11). The Bible also tells us that God gave us joy, peace, and love (Galatians 5:22-23).

One of the ways that we can use our senses, intellect, and emotions is by appreciating art. Art is one of the ways that we can perceive God's beauty and glory, and glorify Him with our lives. Art is one of the ways that we can understand God's truth, grace, and love, and share them with others. Art is one of the ways that we can enjoy God's presence, grace, and joy, and praise Him with our lips.

The Bible gives us many examples of people who appreciated art for God's glory and their good. For example, in Exodus 35, we read about the Israelites, who were God's chosen people. They were freed from slavery in Egypt by God's mighty hand, and they were on their way to the promised land. They were instructed by God to build a tabernacle, a place where God would dwell among them. They brought their offerings of gold, silver, bronze, wood, stone, fabric, and precious stones to the Lord. They also brought their artistic skills and talents to the Lord. They saw the artistic works that Bezalel, Oholiab, and the other craftsmen made for the tabernacle, and they appreciated them. They saw God's art as a sign of His favor, presence, and covenant with them.

Another example is in 1 Kings 10, we read about the Queen of Sheba, who was a wealthy and powerful ruler of a distant land. She heard about the fame and wisdom of King Solomon, and she wanted to see it for herself. She came to Jerusalem with a large caravan of camels, spices, gold, and precious stones. She saw the palace, the temple, the gardens, and the other artistic works that Solomon had made. She also heard the wisdom that Solomon had spoken. She appreciated them, and she praised God for giving such wisdom and splendor to Solomon. She saw God's art as a testimony of His greatness, majesty, and blessing to Solomon.

Another example is in Luke 2, we read about the shepherds, who were poor and humble workers in the fields.

They were watching over their flocks at night, when an angel of the Lord appeared to them and announced the birth of the Savior, who is Christ the Lord. They were told to go to Bethlehem and see the baby, who was lying in a manger. They went with haste and found Mary, Joseph, and the baby. They also saw a multitude of heavenly hosts, praising God and saying, "Glory to God in the highest, and on earth peace among those with whom he is pleased!" (Luke 2:14). They appreciated them, and they glorified and praised God for what they had seen and heard. They saw God's art as a manifestation of His grace, glory, and salvation to them.

These are just a few examples of people who appreciated art for God's glory and their good. There are many more examples in the Bible and in history of people who used their perception, understanding, and enjoyment to appreciate art. God invites us to appreciate art, because He made us in His image and likeness, and He gave us the ability and the desire to create and appreciate art. He invites us to use our senses, intellect, and emotions for His glory and our good. He invites us to see, hear, touch, smell, and taste His art.

God invites us to participate in His creativity and enjoy His artistry, by creating art and by appreciating art. He is not only the ultimate artist and the source of all beauty, but also the most generous and gracious host and teacher. He shares His art with us, He reveals His art to us, and He invites us to join Him in His art.

How God Equips Us with Artistic Gifts and Talents to Reflect His Image and Likeness

The third thing we need to understand about God and art is that God equips us with artistic gifts and talents to reflect His image and likeness. He is not only the ultimate artist and the source of all beauty, but also the most loving and faithful Father and Friend. He does not leave us alone, but He helps us. He does not expect us to be perfect, but He transforms us. He does not demand us to perform, but He empowers us.

God equips us with artistic gifts and talents to reflect His image and likeness in two ways: by giving us His Spirit and by giving us His grace.

God gives us His Spirit, because He loves us and wants to have a personal, intimate, and eternal relationship with us. He gives us His Spirit, who is the Spirit of truth, grace, and love. He gives us His Spirit, who is the Spirit of wisdom, power, and creativity. He gives us His Spirit, who is the Spirit of life, joy, and peace.

The Bible tells us that God gives us His Spirit when we believe in His Son Jesus Christ, who died for our sins and rose again (John 3:16; Ephesians 1:13-14). The Bible also tells us that God gives us His Spirit to dwell in us, to guide us, and to teach us (John 14:16-17, 26). The Bible also tells us that God gives us His Spirit to produce His fruit in us, such as love, joy, peace, patience, kindness, goodness, faithfulness, gentleness, and self-control (Galatians 5:22-23).

One of the ways that God gives us His Spirit is by giving us different gifts and talents according to His will and grace. The Bible tells us that God gives us His Spirit to empower us to serve Him and others with our gifts and talents (1 Corinthians 12:4-11). The Bible also tells us that God gives us His Spirit to inspire us to create and appreciate art with our gifts and talents (Exodus 31:1-6; 1 Chronicles 15:16; 2 Chronicles 2:13-14). The Bible also tells us that God gives us His Spirit to glorify Him and edify others with our gifts and talents (1 Peter 4:10-11; Ephesians 5:18-20).

God gives us His Spirit, who is the Spirit of creativity, to equip us with artistic gifts and talents to reflect His image and likeness. He gives us His Spirit to help us create and appreciate art with wisdom, power, and love. He gives us His Spirit to help us express ourselves, communicate with others, and worship Him through art.

God also gives us His grace, because He loves us and wants to have a personal, intimate, and eternal relationship with us. He gives us His grace, which is His undeserved favor and unmerited kindness. He gives us His grace, which is His forgiveness, acceptance, and adoption. He gives us His grace, which is His strength, provision, and protection.

The Bible tells us that God gives us His grace through His Son Jesus Christ, who died for our sins and rose again (Ephesians 2:8-9; Titus 3:4-7). The Bible also tells us that God gives us His grace to save us, to sanctify us, and to glorify us (Romans 8:28-30). The Bible also tells us that God gives us His grace to help us in our time of need, to supply us with every good thing, and to enable us to do His will (Hebrews 4:16; Philippians 4:19; Hebrews 13:20-21).

One of the ways that God gives us His grace is by giving us different gifts and talents according to His will and grace. The Bible tells us that God gives us His grace to equip us to serve Him and others with our gifts and talents (Romans 12:6-8; 1 Peter 4:10-11). The Bible also tells us that God gives us His grace to inspire us to create and appreciate art with our gifts and talents (Exodus 35:30-35; 2 Chronicles 2:5-7). The Bible also tells us that God gives us His grace to glorify Him and edify others with our gifts and talents (Colossians 3:16-17; 1 Corinthians 10:31).

God gives us His grace, which is His undeserved favor and unmerited kindness, to equip us with artistic gifts and talents to reflect His image and likeness. He gives us His grace to help us create and appreciate art with faith, hope, and love. He gives us His grace to help us express ourselves, communicate with others, and worship Him through art.

God equips us with artistic gifts and talents to reflect His image and likeness, by giving us His Spirit and by giving us His grace. He is not only the ultimate artist and the source of all beauty, but also the most loving and faithful Father and Friend. He helps us, transforms us, and empowers us.

In this chapter, we have explored three aspects of God and art: how God reveals His beauty and glory through His creation, how God invites us to participate in His creativity and enjoy His artistry, and how God equips us with artistic gifts and talents to reflect His image and likeness.

We have learned that God is the ultimate artist and the source of all beauty. He created the world and everything in it with His wisdom, power, and love. He filled the world with His beauty and glory, and He invites us to enjoy and appreciate His creation. He made us in His image and likeness, and He gave us the ability and the desire to create and appreciate art. He speaks to us through His word and His Spirit, and He uses art to communicate His truth, grace, and love to us. He calls us to worship Him with all our heart, soul, mind, and strength, and He uses art to express our love, gratitude, and praise to Him.

We have also learned that God invites us to participate in His creativity and enjoy His artistry, by creating art and by appreciating art. He is not only the ultimate artist and the source of all beauty, but also the most generous and gracious host and teacher. He shares His art with us, He reveals His art to us, and He invites us to join Him in His art.

We have also learned that God equips us with artistic gifts and talents to reflect His image and likeness, by giving us His Spirit and by giving us His grace. He is not only the ultimate artist and the source of all beauty, but also the most loving and faithful Father and Friend. He helps us, transforms us, and empowers us.

As we continue our journey of exploring God and art, let us pray that God will open our eyes, ears, hearts, and minds to see, hear, feel, and understand His beauty and glory as revealed through His creation, His creativity, and His grace. Let us pray that God will inspire us, challenge us, and enable us to create and appreciate art with wisdom, power, and love. Let us pray that God will use us, bless us, and glorify Himself through our artistic gifts and talents. Amen.

CHAPTER 2

Art as a Form of Worship and Witness

Art is not only a human activity, but also a divine gift. God is the ultimate artist, who created the world and everything in it with beauty, order, and purpose. He made us in his image, and gave us the ability and desire to create art as well. Art is one of the ways we can reflect God's glory, express our faith, and share his love with others.

Expression: Art as a Way of Loving God

Art can be a way of expressing our love, gratitude, and praise to God. When we create art, we are using the talents and resources that God has given us to honor him and celebrate his goodness. We are also responding to his beauty and creativity, which we see in his creation and his word.

The Bible is full of examples of people who used art to worship God. For instance, King David composed many psalms, which are songs of praise, thanksgiving, lament, and petition. He also played the harp and danced before the Lord with all his might (2 Samuel 6:14). He said, "I will praise you, Lord, with all my heart; I will tell of all the marvelous things you have done" (Psalm 9:1).

Another example is Bezalel, who was filled with the Spirit of God and given skill, ability, and knowledge in all kinds of crafts. He was the chief artisan of the tabernacle, the sacred tent where God's presence dwelled among his people. He made the ark of the covenant, the altar, the lampstand, and other furnishings, according to God's design and instructions (Exodus 31:1-11). He used gold, silver, bronze, wood, stone, and fabric to create beautiful and meaningful objects that glorified God and served his people.

We can also use art to express our love for God in our own lives. We can sing songs of praise, write poems of gratitude, paint pictures of his grace, sculpt images of his power, and so on. We can use any form of art that suits our personality, culture, and context. The important thing is that we do it with sincerity, humility, and joy, and that we offer it to God as a sacrifice of praise (Hebrews 13:15).

Communication: Art as a Way of Loving Others

Art can also be a way of communicating God's truth, grace, and love to others. When we create art, we are not only expressing ourselves, but also sharing a message with our audience. We are inviting them to see what we see, feel what we feel, and think what we think. We are also challenging them to respond to God's revelation, invitation, and transformation.

The Bible shows us how art can be used to communicate God's message to others. For example, Jesus often used parables, which are stories with a spiritual meaning, to teach his disciples and the crowds. He used familiar images and situations, such as a sower, a seed, a lamp, a treasure, a shepherd, a sheep, and so on, to illustrate the mysteries of the kingdom of God. He said, "Anyone with ears to hear should listen and understand" (Matthew 13:9).

Another example is the apostle Paul, who used poetry, quotations, and references from the culture of his audience to convey the gospel. He quoted from Greek poets and philosophers, such as Aratus, Epimenides, and Menander, to connect with the people of Athens, who were very interested in learning and debating new ideas. He said, "For in him we live and move and exist. As some of your own poets have said, 'We are his offspring'" (Acts 17:28).

We can also use art to communicate God's message to others in our own situations. We can tell stories of God's work in our lives, use metaphors and symbols to explain God's character and plan, create visual and auditory aids to enhance God's word, and so on. We can use any form of art that is appropriate, relevant, and effective for our audience. The important thing is that we do it with clarity, accuracy, and sensitivity, and that we point to God as the source and goal of our message (1 Peter 4:11).

Inspiration: Art as a Way of Loving Ourselves and Others

Art can also be a way of inspiring, challenging, and edifying ourselves and others. When we create or appreciate art, we are not only expressing or communicating, but also learning and growing. We are opening our minds and hearts to new perspectives, insights, and experiences. We are also stimulating our imagination, creativity, and curiosity.

The Bible encourages us to use art to inspire ourselves and others. For example, the book of Proverbs is a collection of wise sayings, which are often poetic, witty, and memorable. They are designed to teach us how to live wisely, justly, and faithfully in God's world. They say, "The proverbs of Solomon son of David, king of Israel: Their purpose is to teach people wisdom and discipline, to help them understand the insights of the wise" (Proverbs 1:1-2).

Another example is the book of Revelation, which is a vision of the end times, which is full of vivid and symbolic imagery. It is meant to comfort, warn, and motivate us to remain faithful to God and his kingdom, in the midst of trials and temptations. It says, "Write down what you have seen—both the things that are now happening and the things that will happen" (Revelation 1:19).

We can also use art to inspire ourselves and others in our own journeys. We can read, watch, listen to, or create art that helps us to understand God's truth, grace, and love better, that challenges us to apply God's word and will to our lives, that edifies us to grow in God's image and likeness, and that motivates us to serve God's purpose and glory. We can use any form of art that enriches, enlightens, and empowers us and others. The important thing is that we do it with discernment, wisdom, and faith, and that we seek God's guidance and approval in our art (Philippians 4:8).

Art is a wonderful gift from God, and a powerful tool for his kingdom. We can use art to worship God, witness to others, and inspire ourselves and others. We can use art to express our love, gratitude, and praise to God, to communicate God's truth, grace, and love to others, and to inspire, challenge, and edify ourselves and others. We can use any form of art that honors God, serves others, and fulfills us. Let us use our art for God's glory and our good. Amen.

CHAPTER 3

Art as a Means of Transformation and Healing

Art is not only a form of expression, but also a form of communication. Through art, we can convey our thoughts, feelings, beliefs, and experiences to others and to ourselves. Art can also be a powerful tool for transformation and healing, as it can help us grow in our knowledge and experience of God, cope with our emotions, struggles, and wounds, and restore our brokenness and wholeness in Christ.

How art can help us grow in our knowledge and experience of God

God is the ultimate source and creator of all beauty and art. He made the heavens and the earth, and everything in them, with wisdom and skill (Psalm 104:24). He made us in His image, and gave us the ability and desire to create and appreciate art (Genesis 1:26-27). He also revealed Himself to us through His Word, His Son, and His Spirit, which are full of grace and truth (John 1:14, 16-17).

Art can help us grow in our knowledge and experience of God, by drawing us closer to Him and His revelation. Art can inspire us to worship God, as we marvel at His works and attributes (Psalm 19:1-4; Romans 1:20). Art can also help us understand God, as we reflect on His character and actions, and how they relate to our lives (Psalm 119:105; Hebrews 4:12). Art can also help us express our love and gratitude to God, as we offer Him our gifts and talents, and use them for His glory (Exodus 35:30-35; 1 Corinthians 10:31).

Some examples of how art can help us grow in our knowledge and experience of God are:

- Music can help us praise God, as we sing or play songs that exalt His name and celebrate His goodness (Psalm 95:1-2; Ephesians 5:19-20).

- Painting can help us visualize God, as we depict His attributes and deeds, or His creation and creatures, with colors and shapes (Exodus 31:1-5; Revelation 4:1-11).

- Poetry can help us meditate on God, as we use words and images to convey His truth and beauty, or our thoughts and feelings towards Him (Psalm 119:97-104; Philippians 4:8).

- Drama can help us imitate God, as we act out His stories and teachings, or His values and virtues, with gestures and emotions (Luke 15:11-32; Ephesians 5:1-2).

- Sculpture can help us honor God, as we create objects that represent His presence and power, or His symbols and signs, with materials and forms (Exodus 25:10-22; 1 Kings 6:23-28).

How art can help us cope with our emotions, struggles, and wounds

Art is not only a form of communication, but also a form of therapy. Through art, we can express and process our emotions, struggles, and wounds, and find relief and healing. Art can also be a source of comfort and hope, as it can remind us of God's love and promises, and His presence and purpose in our lives.

Art can help us cope with our emotions, struggles, and wounds, by providing us with a safe and healthy outlet for our feelings and experiences. Art can help us release our negative emotions, such as anger, sadness, fear, or guilt, and transform them into positive ones, such as joy, peace, courage, or forgiveness (Psalm 42:1-5; Ephesians 4:26-27, 31-32). Art can also help us face our struggles, such as temptations, trials, or conflicts, and overcome them with God's help and guidance (Psalm 46:1-3; James 1:2-5, 12). Art can also help us heal our wounds, such as trauma, loss, or abuse, and find restoration and wholeness in God's grace and mercy (Psalm 147:3; Isaiah 61:1-3).

Some examples of how art can help us cope with our emotions, struggles, and wounds are:

- Music can help us soothe our emotions, as we listen or play songs that calm our nerves and lift our spirits (Psalm 23:1-6; Colossians 3:15-16).

- Painting can help us express our emotions, as we use colors and shapes to convey our mood and state of mind (Psalm 51:1-12; 1 John 1:9).

- Poetry can help us process our emotions, as we use words and images to explore our feelings and thoughts (Psalm 13:1-6; 2 Corinthians 4:16-18).

- Drama can help us resolve our struggles, as we act out our problems and solutions, or our conflicts and reconciliations, with gestures and emotions (Matthew 18:15-17; Romans 12:17-21).

- Sculpture can help us heal our wounds, as we create objects that symbolize our pain and recovery, or our brokenness and wholeness, with materials and forms (Job 19:25-27; 2 Corinthians 5:17).

How art can help us restore our brokenness and wholeness in Christ

Art is not only a form of therapy, but also a form of ministry. Through art, we can share and witness our brokenness and wholeness in Christ, and invite others to experience His transformation and healing. Art can also be a means of service and mission, as it can edify and encourage the body of Christ, and reach out and evangelize the world.

Art can help us restore our brokenness and wholeness in Christ, by testifying to His work and power in our lives. Art can help us acknowledge our brokenness, as we admit our sinfulness and need for a Savior, and confess our faith and trust in Him (Romans 3:23-24; 10:9-10). Art can also help us celebrate our wholeness, as we rejoice in our salvation and new life in Him, and manifest our gifts and fruits of the Spirit (Romans 6:4; 12:6-8; Galatians 5:22-23).

Some examples of how art can help us restore our brokenness and wholeness in Christ are:

- Music can help us proclaim our brokenness and wholeness, as we sing or play songs that declare His grace and glory, and our repentance and praise (Psalm 32:1-5; 103:1-5).

- Painting can help us illustrate our brokenness and wholeness, as we depict His cross and resurrection, and our death and life in Him, with colors and shapes (1 Corinthians 15:3-4; Galatians 2:20).

- Poetry can help us narrate our brokenness and wholeness, as we use words and images to tell His story and ours, and our journey and destination in Him (John 3:16; Revelation 21:1-5).

- Drama can help us demonstrate our brokenness and wholeness, as we act out His love and sacrifice, and our transformation and obedience in Him, with gestures and emotions (John 13:1-17; 15:12-14).

- Sculpture can help us represent our brokenness and wholeness, as we create objects that signify His presence and power, and our identity and purpose in Him, with materials and forms (Matthew 28:18-20; Ephesians 2:10).

Art is a gift from God, and a gift to God. It is a way of connecting with Him, ourselves, and others. It is a way of healing and growing, serving and witnessing. It is a way of living and loving, in His image and for His glory. May we use art as a means of transformation and healing, and as a way of honoring and worshiping our God and Savior, Jesus Christ. Amen.

*So God created mankind in his own image,
in the image of God he created them; male
and female he created them.*

Genesis 1:27

CHAPTER 4

Art as a Tool for Service and Stewardship

Art is not only a gift from God, but also a responsibility to God. He entrusted us with the ability and opportunity to create and appreciate art, and He expects us to use it for His glory and the good of others. Art can be a tool for service and stewardship, as it can serve God's purposes and plans for our lives and the world, bless, support, and empower others in need, and honor God with our resources, time, and talents.

How art can serve God's purposes and plans for our lives and the world

God has a purpose and a plan for each of us, and for the world He created. He wants us to know Him, love Him, and serve Him, and to share His love and truth with others (Jeremiah 29:11; Matthew 22:37-40). He also wants us to be His agents of transformation and reconciliation, and to participate in His mission of restoring all things to Himself (Romans 12:2; 2 Corinthians 5:18-20). He also wants us to enjoy His creation and creativity, and to reflect His beauty and glory in the world (Psalm 19:1; 1 Corinthians 10:31).

Art can serve God's purposes and plans for our lives and the world, by aligning our will and work with His will and work. Art can help us discover and fulfill God's calling for our lives, as we use our gifts and talents to glorify Him and serve others (Ephesians 2:10; 1 Peter 4:10-11). Art can also help us advance God's kingdom in the world, as we use our creativity and influence to spread His gospel and justice (Matthew 28:18-20; Micah 6:8). Art can also help us enjoy and steward God's creation, as we use our resources and skills to care for and enhance His handiwork (Genesis 1:28; 2:15).

Some examples of how art can serve God's purposes and plans for our lives and the world are:

- Music can help us communicate God's message, as we sing or play songs that convey His truth and grace, and invite others to respond to Him (Psalm 96:1-3; Colossians 3:16).

- Painting can help us appreciate God's creation, as we use colors and shapes to capture His beauty and diversity, and inspire others to admire and protect it (Psalm 104:24-25; Romans 1:20).

- Poetry can help us articulate God's vision, as we use words and images to express His will and ways, and challenge others to follow and obey Him (Psalm 119:105; 2 Timothy 3:16-17).

- Drama can help us illustrate God's story, as we act out His acts and words, and invite others to join and continue His story (Luke 24:27; Hebrews 12:1-2).

- Sculpture can help us celebrate God's presence, as we create objects that remind us of His power and love, and encourage others to worship and trust Him (Exodus 25:10-22; 1 Kings 6:23-28).

How art can bless, support, and empower others in need

God cares for the poor, the oppressed, the marginalized, and the broken. He commands us to love our neighbors as ourselves, and to do good to all people, especially to those who belong to the family of believers (Leviticus 19:18; Galatians 6:10). He also calls us to bear one another's burdens, and to comfort and edify each other (Galatians 6:2; 1 Thessalonians 5:11). He also invites us to share in His compassion and mercy, and to participate in His healing and restoration (Matthew 9:36; 25:34-40).

Art can bless, support, and empower others in need, by showing and sharing God's love and grace with them. Art can help us empathize with others, as we use our imagination and emotions to understand their feelings and situations (Romans 12:15; Hebrews 13:3). Art can also help us encourage others, as we use our words and actions to uplift their spirits and strengthen their faith (Proverbs 12:25; 1 Thessalonians 5:14). Art can also help us equip others, as we use our knowledge and skills to teach them and train them for God's service (2 Timothy 2:2; Ephesians 4:11-13).

Some examples of how art can bless, support, and empower others in need are:

- Music can help us comfort others, as we listen or play songs that soothe their pain and sorrow, and offer them hope and peace (Psalm 42:1-5; 2 Corinthians 1:3-4).
- Painting can help us inspire others, as we use colors and shapes to portray their potential and destiny, and

motivate them to pursue and achieve it (Philippians 1:6; 3:12-14).

- Poetry can help us affirm others, as we use words and images to acknowledge their value and dignity, and celebrate their gifts and contributions (Psalm 139:13-16; Ephesians 2:10).

- Drama can help us empower others, as we act out their stories and testimonies, and honor their struggles and victories (Revelation 12:11; Hebrews 11:1-40).

- Sculpture can help us support others, as we create objects that serve their needs and wants, and enhance their quality and joy of life (Proverbs 31:10-31; Acts 9:36-39).

How art can honor God with our resources, time, and talents

God is the owner and giver of everything we have. He provides us with the resources, time, and talents we need to live and thrive. He also entrusts us with the stewardship of these gifts, and He expects us to use them wisely and faithfully (Psalm 24:1; Matthew 25:14-30). He also rewards us with His approval and blessings, and He promises us an eternal inheritance in His kingdom (Matthew 6:19-21; 25:34).

Art can honor God with our resources, time, and talents, by dedicating and investing them for His glory and the good of others. Art can help us honor God with our resources, as we use our money and materials to support His work and workers, and to meet the needs of His people (Malachi 3:10; 2 Corinthians 9:6-15). Art can also help us honor God with our time, as we use our days and hours to serve His purposes and plans, and to make the most of every opportunity (Psalm 90:12; Ephesians 5:15-17). Art can also help us honor God with our talents, as we use our abilities and skills to express His praise and excellence, and to build up His body and kingdom (Exodus 35:30-35; 1 Peter 4:10-11).

Some examples of how art can honor God with our resources, time, and talents are:

- Music can help us honor God with our resources, as we use our money and instruments to sponsor and produce songs that glorify Him and edify others (1 Chronicles 25:1-8; Philippians 4:14-19).

- Painting can help us honor God with our time, as we use our days and brushes to create and display paintings that reflect His beauty and creativity, and inspire others to admire and worship Him (Psalm 8:1-9; 1 Corinthians 10:31).

- Poetry can help us honor God with our talents, as we use our words and poems to praise and thank Him for His goodness and grace, and to share His gospel and wisdom with others (Psalm 150:1-6; Colossians 3:16-17).

- Drama can help us honor God with our resources, time, and talents, as we use our money, hours, and acting skills to organize and perform plays that tell His story and ours, and to invite others to experience His love and salvation (Luke 15:11-32; Acts 2:1-41).

- Sculpture can help us honor God with our resources, time, and talents, as we use our materials, time, and sculpting skills to make and donate sculptures that represent His presence and power, and to encourage others to trust and obey Him (Exodus 25:10-22; 1 Kings 6:23-28).

Art is a responsibility and a privilege from God, and a responsibility and a privilege to God. It is a way of serving and honoring Him, ourselves, and others. It is a way of fulfilling and enjoying His purposes and plans, His gifts and blessings, His calling and mission. It is a way of living and loving, in His image and for His glory. May we use art as a tool for service and stewardship, and as a way of expressing and sharing our love and gratitude to our God and Savior, Jesus Christ. Amen.

CHAPTER 5

Art as a Celebration of Diversity and Unity

Art is not only a responsibility to God, but also a joy from God. He delights in the diversity and unity of His creation and people, and He invites us to join Him in His celebration. Art can be a celebration of diversity and unity, as it can reflect and appreciate the diversity of God's creation and people, foster and promote the unity of God's family and kingdom, and anticipate and rejoice in the beauty of God's future and eternity.

How art can reflect and appreciate the diversity of God's creation and people

God is the source and maker of all diversity and variety. He created the heavens and the earth, and everything in them, with infinite wisdom and creativity (Psalm 104:24; Isaiah 40:28). He made each creature and object unique and wonderful, with different shapes, colors, sounds, and functions (Genesis 1:20-25; Psalm 139:14). He also made each human being in His image, with different races, cultures, languages, and personalities (Genesis 1:26-27; Acts 17:26-27). He also gave each person different gifts, talents, and passions, to express and enjoy His glory and grace (Romans 12:6-8; 1 Corinthians 12:4-11).

Art can reflect and appreciate the diversity of God's creation and people, by imitating and celebrating His creativity and beauty. Art can help us imitate God's creativity, as we use our gifts and talents to create and appreciate art that reflects His design and diversity, and inspires others to do the same (Exodus 35:30-35; Philippians 4:8). Art can also help us celebrate God's beauty, as we use our art to praise and thank Him for His wonderful works and ways, and to share His love and truth with others (Psalm 150:1-6; Colossians 3:16-17).

Some examples of how art can reflect and appreciate the diversity of God's creation and people are:

- Music can help us reflect and appreciate the diversity of God's sounds, as we use our voices and instruments to mimic and harmonize the sounds of nature and culture, and to express and enjoy the diversity of emotions and experiences (Psalm 98:4-9; Revelation 5:9-10).

- Painting can help us reflect and appreciate the diversity of God's colors, as we use our brushes and paints to capture and blend the colors of the sky and the earth, and to portray and admire the diversity of faces and places (Psalm 19:1-4; Revelation 7:9-10).

- Poetry can help us reflect and appreciate the diversity of God's words, as we use our pens and poems to craft and rhyme the words of different languages and dialects, and to communicate and understand the diversity of thoughts and feelings (Psalm 119:97-104; Acts 2:1-11).

- Drama can help us reflect and appreciate the diversity of God's actions, as we use our bodies and costumes to act and mimic the actions of different animals and people, and to explore and learn from the diversity of stories and lessons (Job 12:7-10; Hebrews 11:1-40).

- Sculpture can help us reflect and appreciate the diversity of God's shapes, as we use our hands and materials to shape and mold the shapes of different objects and creatures, and to display and appreciate the diversity of forms and functions (Genesis 2:19-20; 1 Corinthians 12:12-27).

How art can foster and promote the unity of God's family and kingdom

God is not only the maker of diversity, but also the author of unity. He created everything to work together in harmony and order, according to His will and plan (Psalm 104:19-23; Colossians 1:16-17). He also created human beings to live together in love and peace, as His children and His people (Genesis 2:18; Ephesians 2:19-22). He also sent His Son and His Spirit to reconcile and unite us with Himself and with each other, as His body and His bride (John 17:20-23; Ephesians 4:1-6).

Art can foster and promote the unity of God's family and kingdom, by collaborating and cooperating with His Spirit and His people. Art can help us collaborate with God's Spirit, as we use our gifts and talents to create and appreciate art that reveals His presence and power, and that aligns with His will and word (Exodus 31:1-5; John 14:26). Art can also help us cooperate with God's people, as we use our art to serve and honor His purposes and plans, and to edify and encourage His body and bride (1 Corinthians 12:4-11; Ephesians 5:18-21).

Some examples of how art can foster and promote the unity of God's family and kingdom are:

- Music can help us foster and promote the unity of God's voice, as we use our voices and instruments to sing and play songs that declare His truth and grace, and that invite others to join and respond to Him (Psalm 95:1-2; Colossians 3:16-17).

- Painting can help us foster and promote the unity of God's vision, as we use our brushes and paints to create and display paintings that portray His character and actions, and that inspire others to follow and obey Him (Exodus 31:1-5; Revelation 4:1-11).

- Poetry can help us foster and promote the unity of God's message, as we use our pens and poems to craft and share poems that express His love and wisdom, and that challenge others to love and serve Him (Psalm 119:105; 2 Timothy 3:16-17).

- Drama can help us foster and promote the unity of God's story, as we use our bodies and costumes to act and perform plays that tell His story and ours, and that invite others to join and continue His story (Luke 15:11-32; Hebrews 12:1-2).

- Sculpture can help us foster and promote the unity of God's symbol, as we use our hands and materials to make and donate sculptures that represent His presence and power, and that encourage others to worship and trust Him (Exodus 25:10-22; 1 Kings 6:23-28).

How art can anticipate and rejoice in the beauty of God's future and eternity

God is not only the author of unity, but also the giver of beauty. He created everything to reflect and radiate His beauty and glory, in the present and in the future (Psalm 27:4; 1 Corinthians 15:41-43). He also created human beings to enjoy and share His beauty and glory, in this life and in the next (Psalm 16:11; 2 Corinthians 3:18). He also promised to renew and restore all things to Himself, and to make all things new and beautiful, in His new heaven and new earth (Isaiah 65:17; Revelation 21:1-5).

Art can anticipate and rejoice in the beauty of God's future and eternity, by imagining and expressing His promises and plans. Art can help us imagine God's promises, as we use our gifts and talents to create and appreciate art that depicts His future and eternity, and that inspires others to hope and wait for it (Romans 8:18-25; 2 Peter 3:13). Art can also help us express God's plans, as we use our art to praise and thank Him for His future and eternity, and to share His gospel and invitation with others (Psalm 145:1-13; Revelation 22:17).

Some examples of how art can anticipate and rejoice in the beauty of God's future and eternity are:

- Music can help us anticipate and rejoice in the beauty of God's song, as we use our voices and instruments to sing and play songs that celebrate His victory and praise, and that invite others to sing and rejoice with Him (Revelation 5:9-14; 19:6-8).

- Painting can help us anticipate and rejoice in the beauty of God's city, as we use our brushes and paints to create and display paintings that portray His new Jerusalem and His throne, and that inspire others to long and prepare for it (Revelation 21:9-27; 22:1-5).

- Poetry can help us anticipate and rejoice in the beauty of God's word, as we use our pens and poems to craft and share poems that express His promises and blessings, and that challenge others to trust and obey Him (Psalm 119:49-56; Revelation 22:6-7).

- Drama can help us anticipate and rejoice in the beauty of God's wedding, as we use our bodies and costumes to act and perform plays that illustrate His love and sacrifice, and His marriage and feast, and that invite others to love and celebrate with Him (John 3:16; Revelation 19:7-9).

- Sculpture can help us anticipate and rejoice in the beauty of God's crown, as we use our hands and materials to make and donate sculptures that represent His authority and honor, and His reward and inheritance, and that encourage others to serve and worship Him (Revelation 4:9-11; 22:12-13).

Art is a joy and a privilege from God, and a joy and a privilege to God. It is a way of celebrating and honoring Him, ourselves, and others. It is a way of reflecting and appreciating His diversity and unity, His creativity and beauty, His promises and plans. It is a way of living and loving, in His image and for His glory. May we use art as a celebration of diversity and unity, and as a way of expressing and sharing our joy and gratitude to our God and Savior, Jesus Christ. Amen.

CONCLUSION

How to Cultivate a Biblical Vision for Creativity and Beauty

Art is a gift, a responsibility, and a joy from God. He created us in His image, and gave us the ability and desire to create and appreciate art. He also revealed Himself to us through His Word, His Son, and His Spirit, which are full of grace and truth. He also invites us to join Him in His work and worship, His mission and celebration, His transformation and restoration.

In this book, we have explored how to cultivate a biblical vision for creativity and beauty, by looking at five aspects of art from a Christian perspective:

- Art as a Reflection of God's Image and Glory
- Art as a Means of Transformation and Healing
- Art as a Tool for Service and Stewardship
- Art as a Celebration of Diversity and Unity
- Art as an Anticipation of God's Future and Eternity

We have seen how art can help us know and experience God, express and process our emotions, struggles, and wounds, serve and honor God and others, reflect and appreciate God's diversity and unity, and anticipate and rejoice in God's future and eternity. We have also seen how art can inspire and challenge us to grow in our faith, love, and obedience, and to share God's love and truth with others.

We have also learned some practical tips and examples on how to use different forms of art, such as music, painting, poetry, drama, and sculpture, to glorify God and edify others. We have also learned how to use our gifts and talents, our resources and time, our imagination and emotions, our words and actions, to create and appreciate art that honors God and blesses others.

We hope that this book has encouraged and equipped you to cultivate a biblical vision for creativity and beauty, and to use art as a way of living and loving, in God's image and for His glory.

As we conclude this book, let us pray together:
Heavenly Father, thank You for the gift of art. Thank You for creating us in Your image, and giving us the ability and

desire to create and appreciate art. Thank You for revealing Yourself to us through Your Word, Your Son, and Your Spirit, which are full of grace and truth. Thank You for inviting us to join You in Your work and worship, Your mission and celebration, Your transformation and restoration.

Lord, we ask You to help us cultivate a biblical vision for creativity and beauty. Help us to use art as a way of knowing and experiencing You, expressing and processing our emotions, struggles, and wounds, serving and honoring You and others, reflecting and appreciating Your diversity and unity, and anticipating and rejoicing in Your future and eternity.

Lord, we ask You to help us use our gifts and talents, our resources and time, our imagination and emotions, our words and actions, to create and appreciate art that honors You and blesses others. Help us to use art as a way of growing in our faith, love, and obedience, and sharing Your love and truth with others.

Lord, we ask You to bless our art and our lives, and to use them for Your glory and the good of others. We ask You to fill us with Your Spirit, and to guide us with Your wisdom. We ask You to make us more like Your Son, and to prepare us for Your kingdom. We pray all this in the name of Jesus Christ, our Lord and Savior. Amen.

SPECIAL BONUS

Gain access to all my previous and future

books

For we are God's handiwork, created in Christ Jesus to do good works, which God prepared in advance for us to do." - Ephesians 2:10

www.ingramcontent.com/pod-product-compliance
Lightning Source LLC
Chambersburg PA
CBHW070958290526
45795CB00005B/1691